HOLT McDOUGAL

Psychology
Principles in Practice

HOLT McDOUGAL
a division of Houghton Mifflin Harcourt

Research Activities for Teaching Psychology

The 10 Research Activities for Teaching Psychology are designed to provide students with the opportunity to experience firsthand the process of designing and carrying out a psychological study. These extended, multifaceted projects are designed for students to apply the content of *Holt McDougal Psychology* in the creation of projects that relate to different aspects of psychology. Each research project highlights essential skills of the psychological discipline, including collecting, analyzing, and evaluating data, as well as presenting psychological information in written and oral formats.

The Interview

Before starting the activity, tell students that there are three parts to effective interviews: preparation, interview, and post-interview analysis and report. To organize, implement, and conclude their project, students should follow the five steps laid out below. While going through the steps, students should:

- try to prevent their own theories, values, and biases from interfering in the research process,
- use careful and correct reasoning in drawing conclusions from their data, and
- carry out their research in an organized and methodical manner.

STEP 1
FORMING A RESEARCH QUESTION

Tell students that the first step in the research process involves selecting a topic for study. The focus of this activity is the impact of technology on learning. Students should be directed to limit the scope of their research to a particular innovation or group of innovations. For example, students might look at the impact of the Internet.

Once students have selected their topic, they will need to develop operational definitions of key concepts. You may need to remind students that an operational definition is a definition that is stated in terms of measurable characteristics.

Review the Literature

Once students have defined their topic, they need to research what other people have written on the subject. To determine how others have approached the study of the impact of technology on learning and what conclusions they have reached, students will need to review the published reports of studies that have a bearing on the research topic they select. For example, if the topic chosen is "the influence of the Internet," students could look at the writings of educational psychologists.

Discuss with students why good research is conducted within the context of an existing body of knowledge. Note that research will not only provide students with insights but also will help avoid unnecessary duplication of research efforts. Reviewing the literature may also help students redefine their topic or limit the scope of their research. Encourage students to make appropriate adjustments as they work through the five steps.

Suggested readings for this topic include:

Forsyth, Ian (2001), *Teaching & Learning Materials & the Internet.*

Feldman, Alan (2000), *Network Science, a Decade Later: the Internet and Classroom Learning.*

Hird, Anne (2000), *Learning from Cyber-Savvy Students: how Internet-Age Kids Impact Classroom Teaching.*

Ryan, Steve (2000), *The Virtual University: the Internet and Resource-Based Learning.*

Haughey, Margaret Lagan (1998), *Networked Learning: the Pedagogy of the Internet.*

Warshauer, Mark (1995), *E-mail for English Teaching: Bringing the Internet and Computer Learning Networks into the Language Classroom.*

French, Deanie (1999), *Internet Based Learning: an Introduction and Framework for Higher Education and Business.*

STEP 2
FORMING A HYPOTHESIS

After students have reviewed the existing literature, they need to develop a testable hypothesis. The hypothesis should be:

- a statement that predicts the relationship between two or more variables,
- stated clearly and simply, using appropriate terminology
- testable, and
- limited in scope and able to be expressed in a sentence.

Share the following examples of hypotheses with students:

- Most students use the Internet primarily as a learning tool

- A lack of readily available Internet access prevents many students from using the Internet as a learning tool

STEP 3
TESTING THE HYPOTHESIS

Tell students that the next step in the research process involves selecting their research design, or a plan for collecting, analyzing, and evaluating data. Point out that not all research problems lend themselves to every data collection technique, so selecting the correct research design is extremely important. Most of the data-collection methods used by psychologists fall into four categories: surveys, experiments, observation studies, and the analysis of existing sources.

For this project, students will use the survey method, focusing on the interview. Explain to students that during an interview the researcher speaks directly to the respondent. The respondents provide oral answers to the questions. Discuss with the students the reasons they should use the interview method for their research on the impact of technology on learning. You may want to go over some of the issues regarding sampling with students.

Why Use the Interview Method?

- It allows researchers to collect data on attitudes and opinions from large numbers of people.

- Researchers can administer the interviews in person or over the telephone.

- This technique has the advantage of making it easier for researchers to determine whether the respondents understand the questions.

- Researchers can ask for clarification and note various context clues, such a facial expressions, hesitation, or side comments.

Gathering Samples

Ask students what some of the challenges might be in selecting the people to question for the interview. Point out that unless a population is very small, it is impractical to have everyone in the population respond to a survey.

Psychologists generally survey a sample of a population, which is a small number of people drawn from a larger population. Explain that for a sample to be useful, it must be representative of the population from which it was drawn. To help ensure representativeness, psychologists generally rely on random samples, which are chosen in such a way that every member of the population has an equal chance of being included.

Once students understand the issues involved in interviewing, they are ready to begin preparing for the interview. Have students execute the following steps:

Prepare for the Interview

- **Identify the topic.** Students should determine what information is needed and from whom the information may be obtained.

- **Research the topic.** Next, students need to gather available information on the topic from which to base the questions. For example they may look at data relating to Internet access in recent years.

- **Schedule the interview.** Students should identify themselves and clearly state the purpose of the interview. They should also arrange a time when the interview can be conveniently scheduled.

- **Prepare the questions.** Students should devise questions that will draw forth the information they need. Suggest that they group the questions into categories and determine a direction for the interview so that one question leads logically to the next.

- *Open questions* require the respondent to answer the question in his or her own words, allowing an opinion or intensity of feeling to be given. For example: "I use the Internet for: _______________________."

These questions allow freedom of expression and have their place in more qualitative surveys, but they are difficult and time-consuming to code.

- *Closed questions* are more suited to a survey. Discuss the main types of closed questions with the student.

- *Background questions* are used to gather demographic information, such as age and gender.

- *Dichotomous questions* offer only two choices. For example: "Do you have Internet access at home?" (YES/NO), or "I never study on-line." (TRUE/FALSE).

- *Multiple choice questions* offer three or more choices. For example: "How often do you use the Internet to study?" (daily/weekly/monthly).

- With *ranking questions,* the respondent is asked to rank each option that applies. This allows the researcher to obtain information such as relative preferences or importance. For example: "Please indicate, in rank order, the Internet activity you perform most often. Put 1 next to the most popular through to 5 next to the least popular."

  Send e-mail
  Search Web
  Study
  Use chatroom
  Download files

- *Intensity, or Likert scale, statements* allow the respondent to express degrees of agreement / disagreement. For example: "Schools should require students to take tests on-line."
  strongly agree / agree / neither agree nor disagree / disagree / strongly disagree

Pre-Test and Pilot Survey

Tell students that before they conduct the interview, they should carry out a pilot survey. There are a number of reasons why it is important to pre-test an interview:

- To test how long it takes to complete

- To check that the instructions are clear

- To check that the questions are unambiguous

- To check the validity of the questions—are they asking for the correct or relevant information?

- To allow students to eliminate questions that do not yield usable or relevant data

- To allow students to test the coding of the questions

Tell students to pre-test the interview on five or six people from the same population as the final respondents.

After the pilot, tell the students to ask their testers:

- Were the instructions clear?

- Were any questions unclear or ambiguous?

- Did you understand what you were asked?

- Did you object to answering any questions?

- Any other comments?

In light of any problems or comments from the pilot, adjust the interview questions accordingly.

Collect the Data

Discuss with students the importance of following the research design in collecting the data. Point out that different research designs require taking different factors into consideration. Tell students that, regardless of the method being used, they must carefully record the information because careless data collection can affect the accuracy of research findings. Note that students should follow these guidelines to collect the data using the interview method.

Conduct the Interview

- Remind students to explain again to the subject the purpose of the interview, to ensure that the students have the subject's cooperation. Tell the students to indicate how the subject has been chosen—for example, by random sample.

- Remind students to be active listeners, paying close attention to the responses and interaction when appropriate. It is important that the students do not lead or prompt the interviewee in any way, either verbally or by gesture or expression, as this may change the results of the interview, making it inaccurate.

- Remind students to make sure each respondent is asked exactly the same questions in exactly the same way. The structured interview is supposed to reduce the likelihood of this happening, but research reveals that the smallest variation can effect responses.

- Students must record the response accurately. This can be done most easily through the use of tape recorders. Remind students that if they use a tape recorder, they must make sure to receive permission from the subject before they begin.

Write the Oral History

- Advise students to accurately transcribe the information collected in the recorded interview. Code the data carefully: Transcription errors can invalidate the survey.

STEP 4
ANALYZING THE RESULTS

Once students have finished conducting the interview, they are ready to begin analyzing their data. This stage involves two steps:

- **Decoding interview information and data input**

This step involves using the coding scheme by which the students ascribed a numerical value to each response to the interview in the preparatory design phase of the assignment. The students should have already tested the coding in the pilot study, so now they are ready to decode the finished survey. Ensure that the students know how to enter the coding values into the matrix of their statistical software or spread-sheet. Remind them it is essential they input the values accurately and that one entry error will invalidate all subsequent analysis. At the end of the data input, students should understand how the information from their interview has been turned into raw numerical data and be ready to progress to the next step.

- **Statistical analysis data**

Discuss with the students how descriptive statistics can organize information and summarize patterns of responses; for example, the average age of respondents or the number of respondents who have Internet access. Show how frequency and contingency tables will allow them to make statements such as "43 percent of respondents have Internet access.

Ensure that students understand the measures of central tendency—the mode, the mean, and the median—and appreciate the usefulness of being able to describe the data as a single value. It is essential that students understand that identifying and understanding the causal connections between events is a central theme of their research. Psychologists study cause and effect by examining the relationships among variables. A causal relation exists when a change in one variable—the independent variable—produces a change in another variable—the dependent variable. Ensure that the students are able to identify the variables involved in their own research.

STEP 5
PRESENT CONCLUSIONS

Once students have finished analyzing the data, they are ready for the last step in the research process—drawing conclusions from the data and presenting the research findings to others. The conclusions can be presented in numerous ways, but the most useful ways of presenting their data on this topic is through the use of bar charts, pie charts, sociograms, and Venn diagrams. As a class, discuss why psychologists generally report their findings in professional journals, in scholarly books, and at professional meetings. Point out that by reporting their research findings, psychologists add to the body of psychological knowledge and make it possible for other psychologists to evaluate the data and the research process. Note that when sociologists do not supply enough information to allow their research to be repeated by other psychologists, the findings are often viewed as spurious.

Assignment: Ask students to present their findings in a written report. Tell them to describe how they designed the interview, structured the questions, analyzed the data, and drew their conclusions.

Before starting the activity, tell students that although reviewing the literature is one of the major steps in the process of conducting original research, it can also be the sole focus of a research activity. There are three parts to a stand-alone literature review: identifying appropriate literature, reading the literature, and drawing conclusions based on readings. Students can organize, implement, and conclude their project, using the five steps laid out below.

STEP 1
FORMING A RESEARCH QUESTION

Tell students that the first step in the research process involves selecting a topic for study. The focus of this activity is psychoanalysis, for example, the use of psychoanalysis by mental health professionals today.

Once students have selected their topic, they must develop operational definitions of key concepts. Remind students that an operational definition is a definition that is stated in terms of measurable characteristics.

Review the Literature

Once students have defined their topic, they must research published literature reviews. Discuss with students why good research is conducted within the context of an existing body of knowledge. Note that research will provide students with insights and will help avoid unnecessary duplication of research efforts. Reviewing the literature may also help students redefine their topic or limit the scope of their research. Encourage students to make adjustments as they work through the steps.

Suggested readings for this topic include:

Console, W. (1976), *The first encounter: the beginnings in psychotherapy*

Reuben, F. (1990), *Love and work: the value system of psychoanalysis*

Colby, K. (1988), *Cognitive science and psycho-analysis*

Roazen, P. (1990), *Encountering Freud: the politics and histories of psychoanalysis*

Kubie, L. (1975), *Practical and theoretical aspects of psychoanalysis*

STEP 2
FORMING A HYPOTHESIS

The formation of a formal hypothesis normally comes at the conclusion of a literature review, but the student should formulate specific research questions at an early stage in the research in order to narrow down the topic to particular areas of interest. For example, in the study of psychoanalysis, a student might wish to examine how prevalent psychoanalytical methods are among psychologists today.

STEP 3
TESTING THE HYPOTHESIS

Tell students that the next step in the research process involves selecting their research design, or a plan for collecting, analyzing, and evaluating data. Point out that not all research problems lend themselves to every data collection technique, so selecting the correct research design is extremely important. Most of the data-collection methods used by psychologists fall into four categories: surveys, experiments, observation studies, and the analysis of existing sources. For this project students will use the analysis of existing sources method. Discuss with students the reasons they should use the literature review method for their research in the area of psychoanalysis.

Why Use the Literature Review Method?

- It provides the foundation for the study of a particular area and allows the researcher access to secondary sources of information that would be otherwise unavailable.

- It allows the researcher not only to describe the work done in a particular area, but also to evaluate it by identifying contradictions, gaps and inconsistencies in the literature.

- It allows the researcher to narrow down and define a particular area of interest in the topic under consideration and formulate questions that need further research.

Organizing the Literature Review

Tell students that a literature review is not simply a list of existing studies, but should show both relevant information and critical appraisal. Advise students that the literature review should answer a number of questions:

- What do we already know about the area being studied?
- What are the characteristics of the key concepts?
- What are the relationships between these key concepts?
- What are the existing theories?
- What are the shortcomings in these existing theories?

Tell students there are a number of general structures for a review:

- Comparing and contrasting information, in which the researcher describes one area of concern, compares and contrasts it with another, and reflects on what can be learned from the new angle.
- Possible solution structure, in which the researcher considers definitions and solutions, considers alternatives, and summarizes the problem.
- Cause-and-effect structure, in which the researcher describes and clarifies problems, focuses attention on possible causes of the problems, and suggests further research.
- Problem awareness structure, in which the researcher describes the problems with existing research, shows the relevance and the consequences of the problem, and recommends further research to solve the problems.

Once students understand the issues, they are ready to carry out the literature review. Have students execute the following steps:

Prepare for the Literature Review

- **Identify the topic of interest.** In this case, the topic is psychoanalysis. Students should narrow down the topic and pose research questions as a starting point for their research, such as why some psychologists practice psychoanalysis while others do not.

- **Identify the sources of information and where these may be obtained.** It is impossible to read every study written on the topic; the idea is not to summarize all the published work, but to select the most relevant and significant works.

- **Read around the topic area but keep focused on the question or subtopic.** For example, in a study of the use of psychoanalysis, it may be advisable to become familiar with some of Carl Jung's theories.

- **Check the validity of the sources.** For example, identify the writer's purpose and examine the writing for bias, impartiality, or imbalance. Does the study present only one side of an argument, over-simplify complex issues, or present opinions as facts? Who has paid for or published the study, and could this cause bias or prejudice?

Collect the Data

Discuss with students the importance of following the research design in collecting the data. Point out that different research designs require taking different factors into consideration. Tell students that, regardless of the method being used, they must carefully record the information because careless data collection can affect the accuracy of research findings.

Note that to collect the data in the literature review method, students should follow these guidelines:

- List key terms to guide research.
- Jot down key facts that will help to structure information.
- Identify the major ideas. Carefully read the information presented, observing the headings for each of the major ideas or main topics.
- Identify categories and supporting details. Find the major categories under which material is organized. Look for key words that point to supporting details.

- Read the article carefully to identify the main ideas and supporting details. Read the footnotes, endnotes, and bibliography.

- Keep references. Students must present full references to any study they do. Where possible, give the names of researchers, the date of the study, the title of the study, and the source publication.

Conduct the Review

Have students follow the bulleted points:

- **Extract** relevant information from the readings.

- Produce a **critical appraisal** of the information.

- **Use** the information to answer research questions or to narrow and redefine areas for more research or formulating a hypothesis. An initial research question might deal with the prevalence of psychoanalysis today. After reviewing the literature, that area might be redefined and focused on why many psychologists do not use psychoanalysis in their practices.

Write a Summary

- Write a summary describing the main points found in the readings.

STEP 4
ANALYZING THE RESULTS

Remind students that analysis of information collected from a literature review depends on logical organization and rational interpretation of the existing arguments in the area of study. Tell students to be aware of the methodologies used to arrive at the information in the studies and to understand any descriptive statistics used by secondary sources to present data.

STEP 5
PRESENT CONCLUSIONS

Once students have finished analyzing the data, they are ready for the last step in the research process—drawing conclusions from the data and presenting the research findings to others. In presenting conclusions, students should be able to pose and answer a number of questions:

- Does the conclusion address the initial research questions?

- Is the conclusion clear?

- Does the conclusion accurately summarize the main ideas that can be drawn from the information?

- Is the conclusion supported by the existing information?

- Can the conclusion be better presented as a hypothesis and is further research needed to prove or disprove it?

Assignment: Have students present their findings in a written report.

Before starting the activity, tell students that content analysis is a technique used to analyze existing sources. To organize, implement, and conclude their project, students should follow the five steps laid out below.

STEP 1
FORMING A RESEARCH QUESTION

Tell students that the first step in the research process involves selecting a topic for study. The focus of this activity is gender stereotyping in mass media. Students might research the roles assigned to women or men in magazine advertising, television programs, or newspaper comic strips. Encourage students to consider limiting their research by time or publication.

Once students have selected their topic, they will need to develop operational definitions of key concepts. You may need to remind students that an operational definition is a definition that is stated in terms of measurable characteristics. If the concept to be measured is gender stereotypes, an operational definition might be "a set of rigid, discriminatory beliefs arising from a confusion of sex roles and gender roles which categorize men and women according to cultural construct and social expectation and promote the belief that these differences are biological."

Review the Literature

Once students have defined their topic, they need to research what other people have written on the subject. To determine how others have approached the study of gender stereotyping in mass media and what conclusions they have reached, students will need to review the published reports of studies that have a bearing on the research topic they select.

Suggested readings for this topic include:

Meehan, Diana M. (1983). *Ladies of the Evening: Women Characters of Prime-time Television*

Smith, Lois J. (1994). "A Content Analysis of Gender Differences in Children's Advertising" (*Journal of Broadcasting & Electronic Media*, 38[3])

Dines, Gail, and Humez, Jean M. (eds.) (1994). *Gender, Race, and Class in Media: A Text-reader*

Goffman, Erving (1979). *Gender Advertisements*

Craig, Steve (ed) (1992). *Men, Masculinity and the Media*

Gunter, Barrie (1995). *Television and Gender Representation*

Macdonald, Myra (1995). *Representing Women: Moral of Femininity in the Popular Media*

LaRossa, R. (2001). "Gender Disparities in Mother's Day and Father's Day Comic Strips: A 55 Year History" (*Sex Roles: A Journal of Research*)

Kaufman, G. (1999). "The Portrayal of Men's Family Roles in Television Commercials (statistical data included)" (*Sex Roles: A Journal of Research*)

Lin, C. A. (1998). "Uses of Sex Appeal in Prime-time Television Commercials" (*Sex Roles: A Journal of Research*)

Courtney, A., and Whipple, T. (1983). *Sex Stereotyping in Advertising*

McCracken, Ellen (1993). *Decoding Women's Magazines: From Mademoiselle to Ms.*

STEP 2
FORMING A HYPOTHESIS

After students have reviewed the existing literature, they need to develop a testable hypothesis. The hypothesis should be a statement that predicts the relationship between two or more variables.

Share the following examples of hypotheses with students:

- Soap operas negatively affect women by portraying them as the weaker sex.

- Magazine advertisements tend to show women as housewives and men as head of the household.

- Television commercials aimed at children are likely to use assumptions of stereotypical gender roles.

STEP 3
TESTING THE HYPOTHESIS

Tell students that the next step in the research process involves selecting their research design, or a plan for collecting, analyzing, and evaluating data. Point out that not all research problems lend themselves to every data collection technique, so selecting the correct research design is extremely important. Most of the data-collection methods used by psychologists fall into four categories: surveys, experiments, observation studies, and the analysis of existing sources.

For this project students will use the content analysis method. Discuss with students the reasons they should use the content analysis method for their research on gender stereotyping in mass media.

Content analysis is a research tool commonly used in the study of media, although it has application across a wide range of disciplines. It is used to determine the presence of certain concepts within text, and then quantify and analyze the frequency and meanings of those concepts. Researchers can then go on and draw inferences from their analysis about the writer, the audience, and the culture of the time the text was produced.

At its most basic, content analysis is a straightforward statistical exercise that involves categorizing an aspect or quality of behavior and counting the number of times such behavior occurs.

- A basic content analysis of a newspaper might count the number of column inches given to information about men as opposed to information about women.

- A basic content analysis of a television show might simply count the number of times the focus was on male characters as opposed to the times the focus was on women characters.

A more complex content analysis would attempt to give meaning and context to the concepts it was measuring.

- A complex content analysis of a newspaper might examine the prominence and slant given to the information about men and women. For example, does the front page feature a positive story about men and a negative one about women and how might this affect women?

- A complex content analysis of a television show might give more detail and look at the context and background of the occurring concepts. For example, where is the character most seen (at home? at work?) and what does the character do (cook meals? drive? play a sport?)?

The two types of content analysis are:

- **Conceptual Analysis.** Concepts are chosen for examination and the researcher is interested in only counting, or quantifying, their presence, not in examining relationships between them. This type produces quantitative data.

- **Relational Analysis.** This type goes further and examines the relationships between concepts. Individual concepts are seen as having no meaning in isolation. Often, semantics (the study of the meaning of words) and semiotics (the study of the meaning of symbols and signs) are used to find the meaning that is the product of the relationships between concepts. This type relies on interpretations of meaning and produces qualitative data.

Sophisticated content analysis can help the researcher build up a picture of what lies beneath the interaction on the surface: the patterns of behavior, social assumptions, and cultural context. Ask the students to study Diane Meehan's *Ladies of the Evening,* a 1983 content analysis of the way women were portrayed in prime time television drama shows. She discussed how women were shown as one-dimensional rather than as complex personalities: They were portrayed as either good or bad. Good women were those content to play supportive, domesticated roles, submissive to men; bad women were independent, but also had selfish, aggressive, and destructive characteristics. Using a systematic approach to looking at female relationships, Meehan was able to demonstrate how assumptions about women are often hidden from view.

Why Use the Content Analysis Method?

- Content analysis is relatively cheap, simple, and easy to carry out.

- Using a standardized grid, complex forms of interaction can be coded into manageable categories, reducing the text to an easily quantified set of data.

- It can reveal the way written and recorded documents encourage the reader and viewer to see something in a particular way.

- It can provide an objective, quantified account of themes, issues, and so forth, and provide insights into aspects of cultural communications that are not always obvious to the reader or viewer.

- It is an unobtrusive research method, and, unlike surveys and observation, does not depend on other people's responses, reducing the possibilities of spoiled or biased data.

The most basic tool of content analysis is an analysis grid: a chart divided into the categories of behavior and the variables the researcher is studying. Using the grid, the researcher is able to collect information easily and systematically.

Prepare for the Content Analysis

- **Define the topic.** In this case, the area is gender stereotypes in the media. Ensure that the students have a broad knowledge of the indicators they will be looking for: They should draw up an operational list of common gender stereotypes and reduce them to categories. For example, Social (male is the family breadwinner, female is the nurturing caregiver), Occupational (male is the executive, engineer, doctor; female is secretary, teacher, nurse, housewife); Emotional (male is strong, aggressive; female is passive, weak).

- **Determine the extent of the analysis.** For example, students choosing the children's commercial activity might determine to videotape an hour of Saturday morning television, rich in children's commercials.

- **Prepare a content analysis grid.** Discuss with students the format of their grid and the categories they will use to quantify indicators of gender stereotypes. For example, to analyze commercials, students might note the product, the sex of the main character, the activity of the character, the sex of the voice-over, and the setting of the commercial.

Collect the Data

Discuss with students the importance of following the research design in collecting the data. Point out that different research designs require taking different factors into consideration. Tell students that, regardless of the method being used, they must carefully record the information because careless data collection can affect the accuracy of research findings. Note that students will follow these guidelines to collect the data for content analysis.

Analyze the Content

- **Initial scrutiny.** Students should examine or watch their subject matter closely before filling in the grid. Encourage them to make notes on little-noticed elements, such as the type of music in commercials or the typeface used in printed advertisements.

- **Fill in the analysis grid.** Tell the students to take as much care filling in the grid as they would in collecting data for any other research method.

- **Reduce and reorganize the categories.** Once the analysis grid is complete, it can be used to reorganize the data in a number of ways. For example, products could be grouped as types, such as toys, food, or candy, or settings could be grouped as in the home, out of doors, or fantasy setting.

Reliability of Content Analysis

- Discuss with the students the reliability of content analysis data. Point out that in some instances it might be questionable since it involves the researcher making judgments about the categorization of concepts.

STEP 4
ANALYZING THE RESULTS

Remind students that the purpose of their data analysis is to determine whether the data support their research hypothesis. For example, if students find that children's commercials use underlying notions of traditional gender roles, the hypothesis is proven.

Statistical analysis involves analyzing data that have already been collected to determine the strength of the relationship that may exist between two or more variables. A variable is a characteristic that can differ from one individual, group, or situation to another in a measurable way. Ensure that students understand the relationship of the variables in the content analysis to the categories that were used.

Students should understand how descriptive statistics will allow them to organize and summarize the data. They should be familiar with two basic statistical concepts: the frequency distribution and the three measures of central tendency: the mode, the mean, and the median. These concepts will allow the students to make generalizations about the data.

For instance, a frequency distribution will show how often a particular score occurs. In this case, a score may be the number of gender indicators occurring in a commercial.

Using a measure of central tendency, students will be able to find out the number of, say, female gender indicators that is most representative of the number of female gender indicators occurring in every commercial.

A measure of central tendency is a statistical average—a single value—that describes the data under consideration. Measures of central tendency can be calculated on any set of data as long as the data can be translated into numbers.

The same data will produce different averages depending on which of the three measures of central tendency is used. The mean is the measure obtained by adding up all the numbers in the data and dividing that number by the total number of cases. This is the measure that we most often think of when we think of averages. For example, the student has analyzed 10 commercials and ascribed a score of female gender indicators for each:

4, 2, 5, 1, 3, 5, 1, 2, 2, 4

The mean score is 29/10 = 2.9

The median is the number, or value, that divides the range of data into two equal parts:
The median = 3 because there are two above it and two below it—it divides the range.
The mode is the number that occurs most often in the data:
The mode = 2 because it occurs three times.

Identifying and understanding the causal connections between events is a central theme in research. Psychologists study cause and effect by examining the relationships among variables. A causal relation exists when a change in one variable produces a change in another variable. Psychologists, like other scientists, use special terms to identify cause-and-effect variables. The cause—the variable that produces the changes in the second variable—is called the independent variable. The effect—the variable that is altered by the presence of the independent variable—is called the dependent variable.

Once students have analyzed the information gathered using the content analysis method, they should prepare a summary of the information.

STEP 5
PRESENT CONCLUSIONS

Once students have finished analyzing the data, they are ready for the last step in the research process—drawing conclusions from the data and presenting the research findings to others. Ensure that the students address the hypothesis and encourage them to look for other relationships, such as "commercials with male voice-overs are likely to be aimed at boys" or "commercials set inside the home are more likely to feature girls as the main characters."

Assignment: Have students present a written report to the class. See Activity 10, "The Presentation."

Before starting the activity, tell students that there are three parts to the historical method: identify the topic to be examined, collect the data, and data analysis. To organize, implement, and conclude their project, students should follow the seven steps laid out below. While going through the steps, students should:

- try to prevent their own theories, values, and biases from interfering in the research process,

- use careful and correct reasoning in drawing conclusions from their data, and

- carry out their research in an organized and methodical manner.

STEP 1
FORMING A RESEARCH QUESTION

Tell students that the first step in the research process involves selecting a topic for study. Students might research how treatment techniques for persons suffering from mental illness have changed over time. Students should be directed to limit the scope of their research to a particular medium and time period. For example, students might look at how treatment changed during the 1800s and 1900s.

Once students have selected their topic, they will need to develop operational definitions of key concepts. You may need to remind students that an operational definition is a definition that is stated in terms of measurable characteristics.

Review the Literature

Once students have defined their topic, they need to research what other people have written on the subject. Students will need to review the published reports of studies that have a bearing on the research topic they select.

Discuss with students why good research is conducted within the context of an existing body of knowledge. Note that research will not only provide students with insights but also will help avoid unnecessary duplication of research efforts. Reviewing the literature may also help students redefine their topic or limit the scope of their research. Encourage students to make

appropriate adjustments as they work through the seven steps.

Suggested readings for this topic include:

Bromberg, Walter (1975), *From Shaman to Psychotherapist: a History of the Treatment of Mental Illness.*

Briggs, L. Vernon (1973), *History of the Psychopathic Hospital, Boston, Massachusetts.*

Gamwell, Lynn (1995), *Madness in America: Cultural and Medical Perceptions of Mental Illness Before 1914.*

Deutsch, Albert (1949), *The Mentally Ill in America: a History of their Care and Treatment from Colonial Times.*

Step 2
FORMING A HYPOTHESIS

After students have reviewed the existing literature, they need to develop a testable hypothesis. The hypothesis should be a statement that predicts the relationship between two or more variables.

Share the following examples of hypotheses with students:

- In the past, treatment techniques for mentally ill persons had little scientific basis.

- Treatment techniques have changed dramatically during the last 100 years.

STEP 3
TESTING THE HYPOTHESIS

Tell students that the next step in the research process involves selecting their research design, or a plan for collecting, analyzing, and evaluating data. Point out that not all research problems lend themselves to every data collection technique, so selecting the correct research design is extremely important. Most of the data-collection methods used by psychologists fall into four categories: surveys, experiments, observation studies, and the analysis of existing sources. For this project students will use the historical method.

The historical method is one of the techniques used to analyze existing sources. It involves examining any materials from the past that contain information of psychological interest. These materials can include written documents, such as diaries, scholarly books, newspapers, magazines, government records, laws, and letters.

The historical method enables researchers to learn about events that happened in the recent past or long ago. It also provides a way to study trends. In the case of personal material, such as letters and diaries, the historical method allows researchers to view the private, unguarded feelings of individuals who lived during another time.

Why Use the Historical Method?

Discuss with students the reasons they should use the historical method for their research.

- It allows researchers to access the materials of the past: personal and private material as well as public and official information. Included as material are films, magazines, and radio recordings.

- As a source of data, it is cheap, convenient and readily available. For instance, to study the treatment of mental illness in the past, scholarly studies on the topic are easily obtained.

- The historical method allows comparative research. Data from the past can be directly compared with today's and relationships identified.

- Researchers can apply modern analytical methods and interpretive tools to historical data and come up with new ways of seeing the past.

Historical Data as a Secondary Source

Historical research involves studying, understanding, and explaining past events in order to arrive at conclusions about causes, effects, or trends of what happened in the past or what may happen in the future. It is not always easy to ensure that the historical sources used are reliable or valid, so the elements to consider are:

- **Authenticity.** Is the source of the data the original document or an altered copy or a forgery?

- **Credibility.** Researchers may want to know who wrote a document, why it was written, and whether or not the writer had firsthand experience of things decribed or was simply repeating hearsay.

- **Representativeness.** Researchers need to know whether the views expressed in a document were one individual's view or the views of several people.

- **Meaning.** Researchers should consider both the literal meaning of the document and the hidden meaning that illustrates a particular sociological point. This is especially relevant when considering a film.

- **Purpose.** Researchers must be aware of the reason the historical document was originally produced.

Once students understand the issues involved in historical method, they are ready to collect the historical data.

Collect the Data

Discuss with students the importance of following the research design in collecting the data. Point out that different research designs require taking different factors into consideration. Tell students that, regardless of the method being used, they must carefully record the information because careless data collection can affect the accuracy of research findings. Note that students should follow these guidelines to collect the data for the historical method.

- **Define the problem.** Ask pertinent questions such as: Is the historical method appropriate? Are pertinent data available? Will the findings be significant?

- **Develop a research framework for the conduct of the research.** Questions focus on
  - **events (who, what, when, where)**
  - **how** an event occurred (descriptive)
  - **why** the event happened (interpretive)

- **Collect the data.** Data collection may consist only of taking many notes and organizing the data. The researcher should code topics and subtopics in order to arrange and file the data.

- **Use external and internal criticism.** The research should evaluate the data. Sources of data include documents (letters, diaries, bills, receipts, newspapers, journals/magazines, films, pictures, recordings, personal and institutional records, and budgets), oral testimonies of participants in the events, and relics (textbooks, buildings, etc.). As well as offering an interpretive analysis of the document, the student could source documents of the same period to strengthen and support the interpretation (for example, psychological texts from the era being studied).

- **Report the findings.** This step includes a statement of the problem, review of source material, assumptions, research questions and methods used to obtain findings, the interpretations and conclusions, and a thorough bibliographic referencing system.

STEP 4
ANALYZING THE RESULTS

Once students have finished collecting data, they are ready to begin analyzing the data. As a class, discuss why the analysis of the data collected is an important step. Point out that even if students used the proper research design and carefully collected data, the accuracy of their findings can be affected by how they analyze the data. Tell students that as researchers, they must be careful to maintain their objectivity and not read more into the data than is there because research findings are only as good as the methods used to collect and analyze the data. Remind students that the purpose of their data analysis is to determine whether the data support their research hypothesis.

In the example given, research would be largely qualitative. If a comparative analysis were to be carried out, however, elements of comparison could be reduced to quantifiable data by content analysis. In this case, the student should be aware of the uses of descriptive statistics to organize and summarize data: frequency distributions and the measure of central tendency, for example.

Once students have analyzed the information gathered using the historical method, they should prepare a summary of the information.

STEP 5
PRESENT CONCLUSIONS

Once students have finished with analyzing the data, they are ready for the last step in the research process—drawing conclusions from the data and presenting the research findings to others.

Assignment: Student should present their findings as an oral report to the class. They may wish to include visuals to accompany their report.

Before starting the activity, tell students that there are three parts to effective observation: choosing a suitable subject to observe, carrying out the observation, and analyzing the data. To organize, implement, and conclude their project, students should follow the five steps laid out below. While going through the steps, students should

- try to prevent their own theories, values, and biases from interfering in the research process,

- use careful and correct reasoning in drawing conclusions from their data, and

- carry out their research in an organized and methodical manner.

STEP 1
FORMING A RESEARCH QUESTION

Tell students that the first step in the research process involves selecting a topic for study. The focus of this activity is adolescents as a social group. Students might research the nature of gender differences in communication, or how high school subgroups or cliques establish separate identities from the wider group.

Once students have selected their topic, they will need to develop operational definitions of key concepts. You may need to remind students that an operational definition is a definition that is stated in terms of measurable characteristics. For example, the operational definition of gender differences would be "inequalities in culturally determined values ascribed to males and females."

Review the Literature

Once students have defined their topic, they need to research what other people have written on the subject. To determine how others have approached the study of communication in adolescents and what conclusions they have reached, students will need to review the published reports of studies that have a bearing on the research topic they select.

Discuss with students why good research is conducted within the context of an existing body of knowledge. Note that research will not only provide students with insights but also will help avoid unnecessary duplication of research efforts. Reviewing the literature may also help students redefine their topic or limit the scope of their research. Encourage students to make appropriate adjustments as they work through the five steps.

Suggested reading for this topic include:

Eckert, Penelope (1989). *Jocks & burnouts: Social Categories and Identity in the High School*

Harris, Cheryl (ed.) (1998). *Theorizing Fandom: Fans, Subculture, and Identity*

Widdicombe, Sue, and Wooffitt, Robin (1995). *The Language of Youth Subculture: Social Identity in Action*

Romain, Trevor (1998), *Cliques, Phonies & Other Baloney.*

Advances in Gender and Communication Research (1987)

Pearson, Judy (1991), *Gender & Communication.*

Wood, Julia (1994), *Gendered Lives : Communication, Gender, and Culture.*

Todd, Alexandra Dundas (1988), *Gender and Discourse : the Power of Talk.*

Eder, Donna (1995), *School Talk: Gender and Adolescent Culture.*

Briton, N. J., and Hall, J. A. (1995). "Beliefs about female and male nonverbal communication" (*Sex Roles: A Journal of Research*)

Muus, Rolf E., (1980). *Adolescent Behavior and Society: A Book of Readings*

Wagner, H. L., Buck, R., and Winterbotham, M. (1993). "Communication of specific emotions: Gender differences in sending accuracy and communication measures" (*Journal of Nonverbal Behavior*)

Wheelan S. A., and Verdi, A. F. (1992). "Differences in male and female patterns of communication in groups: A methodological artifact?" (*Sex Roles: A Journal of Research*)

Burgoon, Judee K., Buller, David B., and Woodall, W. G. (1996). *Nonverbal communication: The unspoken dialogue*

Bucholtz, M. (1999). "'Why be normal?'": Language and identity practices in a community of nerd girls" *(Language in Society)*

Thurlow, C. (2001). *'Talkin' 'bout my communication'—Communication Awareness in Early Adolescence (Language Awareness)*

Tannen, Deborah (2001). *You Just Don't Understand: Women and Men in Conversation*

STEP 2
FORMING A HYPOTHESIS

After students have reviewed the existing literature, they need to develop a testable hypothesis. Although the observation method does not always require an initial hypothesis, here it provides a convenient starting point.

Share the following examples of hypotheses with students:

- Girls are more likely than boys to show their feelings through nonverbal communication.

- Communication within mixed gender adolescent groups is different from that within single gender groups.

STEP 3
TESTING THE HYPOTHESIS

Tell students that the next step in the research process involves selecting their research design, or a plan for collecting, analyzing, and evaluating data. Point out that not all research problems lend themselves to every data collection technique, so selecting the correct research design is extremely important. Most of the data-collection methods used by psychologists fall into four categories: surveys, experiments, observation studies, and the analysis of existing sources.

In observation studies researchers observe the behavior of individuals. The observation method can be either naturalistic or laboratory. In naturalistic observation, researchers observe the situation under study without interfering with it. Because researchers do not participate in the situation being studied, individuals often do not realize that they are being observed. This has the advantage of making it less likely that behavior will be affected by the known presence of a researcher.

For matters that cannot be studied in a natural setting, psychologists sometimes turn to the laboratory-observation method. Carrying out a study in a laboratory often allows researchers to better control the study's environment. For example, a researcher in a laboratory could administer a written or oral test that is designed to provide information about the different ways men and women communicate.

Discuss with the students the reasons they should use the observation method for their research on adolescent communication. Ensure that they understand the unsuitability of quantitative research methods to study adolescent language and group communications. Discuss which type of observation best suits the suggested activities—for example, the gender differences in communication activity is ideal for the naturalistic-observation method.

Why Use the Observation Method?

- Behavior can be directly observed. For example, there is no other way to adequately research teenage group interaction. No matter how willing the teenagers might be to be interviewed or fill in a questionnaire, none of those methods can ever provide a valid picture of the way of life of the subjects.

- The observation method allows the researcher to investigate groups who would not or could not respond to other methods of research, such as children or those engaged in deviant behavior. It also allows a view of individuals' unconscious behavior, such as nonverbal communication, that no other method could investigate.

- *Covert* observation means that the subjects are unaware that they are under investigation, reducing the risk of them modifying their behavior. For instance, if the group of adolescents knew they were being observed, they would be self-conscious and less likely to behave naturally.

- The researchers can directly see events that occur within a group and can gather data that otherwise might not have occurred to them to collect.

Once students understand the issues involved in the observation method, they are ready to begin their observation. Have students execute the following steps:

Prepare for the Observation

- **Identify the topic.** Students should determine what information is needed and from whom the information may be obtained. In this case, the topic is adolescent communications: for convenience, students could observe schoolmates in a natural setting. Discuss with students the implications of observing a familiar group if the participant observation method is chosen.

- **Research the topic.** Next, students need to gather available information on the topic from existing sources. From the literature, students should learn what to look for when they begin the observation. For example, they should learn that communication involves not only speech, but also factors such as body language, personal space, dress, hairstyle, and tone of voice.

- **Identify the group to be observed and where the observation will take place.** If the observation is done in school, it should be at a time when the subjects are able to be relaxed—perhaps in the cafeteria. A research schedule should be negotiated, determining how long the observation will last, how often it will take place, and so on. This will obviously depend on the activity chosen, but there should be at least three observation sessions.

Collect the Data

Discuss with students the importance of following the research design in collecting the data. Point out that different research designs require taking different factors into consideration. Tell students that, regardless of the method being used, they must carefully record the information because careless data collection can affect the accuracy of research findings. Note that students should follow these guidelines to collect the data for the observation method.

Conduct the Observation

- A danger of observation is that the researcher may misinterpret or misunderstand behavior. Students should always be aware that errors of interpretation may bias the research.

- Students should keep a detailed field diary to record data. It may be difficult to take notes openly without alerting the group, so it may be necessary to rely on memory and write down observations at the end of the day. Notes should be extensive, descriptive, and should cover every aspect of the observation—not only details of the subjects, but of the place where the observation occurred, the time of day, and so forth. Sometimes it is useful to take photographs or video footage of the subjects. This may not always be practical or appropriate, especially if the observation is covert. A tape recorder could be another aid to data collection. Discuss the ethical considerations of privacy with the students.

Interpreting the Data

Data collected by this research method may be difficult to interpret and will depend on the skill of the researcher to observe events accurately. The researcher should take care to:

- Make thoughtful and informed decisions on what behavior is insignificant and significant.

- Always be aware that data is based on his or her own subjective interpretation of what is occurring.

STEP 4
ANALYZING THE RESULTS

Once students have finished conducting the observation, they are ready to interpret the data. Unlike the quantifiable methods of research such as structured interviews and questionnaires that seek to reduce the social world to numerical information to be processed, observation is a *qualitative* research method. Qualitative researchers have the belief that to understand behavior, research has to imitate life and become involved in the interactions which create everyday shared meanings of life—hence the technique of studying the group or individual for long periods of time and seeking to understand their behavior, reasoning, and choices in the natural, real-world setting.

Student observers will not have masses of quantifiable data to analyze, but they will have the extensive and detailed notes they made in their field diary, the answers to any questions they managed to ask the subjects, any photographs, drawings, or tape recordings they were able to make, and their memories to process.

The report that will be produced from the researchers' interpretation of this documentation will not seek to prove relationships and causes, but attempt to explain social life by reproducing the experience of the group as a narrative, containing descriptions of crucial events and typical group behavior.

Students should use their field diaries and any other information they recorded to write their report, ensuring that they address the initial hypothesis. Once students have analyzed the information gathered using the observation method, they should prepare a summary of the information.

STEP 5
PRESENT CONCLUSIONS

Once students have finished interpreting the data, they are ready for the last step in the research process—drawing conclusions from the data and presenting the research findings to others. As a class, discuss why psychologists generally report their findings in professional journals, in scholarly books, and at professional meetings. Point out that by reporting their research findings, psychologists add to the body of psychological knowledge and make it possible for other psychologists to evaluate the data and the research process. Note that when psychologists do not supply enough information to allow their research to be repeated by other psychologists, the findings are often viewed as spurious.

Assignment: Have students prepare and deliver an oral presentation to the class. Ask them to include the reasons for choosing this research method, how they prepared for the observation, and the difficulties they encountered. Ask them to address their initial hypothesis. If any photographs or video footage was taken, ask that those be shown these to illustrate key points.

Before starting the activity, tell students that there are four parts to effective questionnaires: (1) *Preparation:* choosing the topic, formulating a hypothesis, studying the literature; (2) *Design:* sampling—who will be surveyed; questionnaire design—turning the objectives of the survey into questions that will give relevant information; (3) *Fieldwork:* administering the questionnaire and collecting the data; (4) *Processing:* coding and inputting data; statistical analysis of data, interpreting the results, drawing conclusions, and writing the report.

To organize, implement, and conclude their project, students should follow the five steps laid out below. While going through the steps, students should:

- try to prevent their own theories, values, and biases from interfering in the research process,

- use careful and correct reasoning in drawing conclusions from their data, and

- carry out their research in an organized and methodical manner.

STEP 1
FORMING A RESEARCH QUESTION

Tell students that the first step in the research process involves selecting a topic for study. The focus of this activity is adolescents and dating behavior. Students might look at whether dating helps teens relate positively to other people, or gender roles within a dating relationship.

Once students have selected their topic, they will need to develop operational definitions of key concepts. You may need to remind students that an operational definition is a definition that is stated in terms of measurable characteristics. In this case, an operational definition of adolescence might refer to "members of the post-pubertal population younger than 20 years of age who have a distinctive lifestyle and are undergoing biological, cognitive, and social transition." Dating behavior can be defined as "engaging in pre-marital social or emotional relationships with a contemporary, often casual, informal, and temporary, sometimes becoming formalized and permanent as marriage."

Review the Literature

Once students have defined their topic, they need to research what other people have written on the subject. To determine how others have approached adolescent dating behavior and what conclusions they have reached, students will need to review the published reports of studies that have a bearing on the research topic they select.

Discuss with students why good research is conducted within the context of an existing body of knowledge. Note that research will not only provide students with insights but also will help avoid unnecessary duplication of research efforts. Reviewing the literature may also help students redefine their topic or limit the scope of their research.

Suggested readings for this topic include:

Waller, Willard (1937). "The Rating & Dating Complex" (*American Sociological Review*)

Gordon, M. *Was Waller Ever Right? The Rating & Dating Complex Reconsidered (Journal of Marriage and the Family, 43)*

Gordon, M. & Miller, R. *Going Steady in the 80s: Exclusive Relationships in Six Connecticut High Schools (Sociology & Social Research, 68)*

Hansen, S. L. *Dating Choices of High School Students (The Family Co-ordinator, 57)*

Sarnet, N., and Kelly, E. W. *The Relationship of Steady Dating to Self-Esteem and Sex Role Identity Among Adolescents (Adolescence, 22)*

Furman, Wyndol, B. Brown, and Candie Fiering (eds.) (1999). *The Development of Romantic Relationships in Adolescence*

Larson and Jensen Campbell. *The Nature and Function of Social Exchange in Adolescent Romantic Relationships*

Elliot, Glen R., and Feldman, Shirley S. (1990). *At The Threshold: The Developing Adolescent*

Grinder, Robert E. (1978). *Adolescence (2nd ed.)*

STEP 2
FORMING A HYPOTHESIS

After students have reviewed the existing literature, they need to develop a testable hypothesis. The hypothesis should be:

- a statement that predicts the relationship between two or more variables,

- stated clearly and simply, using appropriate terminology,

- testable, and

- limited in scope and able to be expressed in a sentence.

Share the following examples of hypotheses for this topic with students:

- Dating helps girls and boys relate to other people.

- Adolescents can attain status through dating.

- Dating relationships are characterized by unequal gender roles.

STEP 3
TESTING THE HYPOTHESIS

Tell students that the next step in the research process involves selecting their research design, or a plan for collecting, analyzing, and evaluating data. Point out that not all research problems lend themselves to every data-collection technique, so selecting the correct research design is extremely important. Most of the data-collection methods used by psychologists fall into four categories: surveys, experiments, observation studies, and the analysis of existing sources.

For this project, students will use the survey method, focusing on the questionnaire. Explain to students that there are two kinds of questionnaires:

- the self-completing questionnaire, where individuals answer the questions privately, without the need for the researcher's presence; also known as the "postal" questionnaire;

- the structured interview, where the researcher reads the questions to the individual and fills in the answers.

Discuss with the students the differences between the two types and point out the advantages of the self-completing questionnaire over the structured interview.

Why Use the Questionnaire?

- It is cheap and relatively easy to distribute to a large number of people. No interviewers have to be present.

- It is reliable. It uses a standardized data-collection design, and so presents the same questions asked in the same order in the same way every time, whereas an interviewer may inadvertently introduce bias into the data by asking the questions inconsistently.

- It can be filled in anonymously and privately, allowing respondents to be frank and honest about personal matters.

- It is easy to process and coding is quick and accurate, and, where closed questions have been used, coding can be incorporated on the questionnaire form itself.

Disadvantages of the self-completing questionnaire are:

- Low response rate—very few are ever returned;

- Respondent might misunderstand or misinterpret the instructions or a question;

- Impossible to check whether the respondent filled it in or gave it to someone else to fill in, or deliberately filled it in incorrectly.

Point out that these potential drawbacks can be minimized by careful design and construction of the questionnaire and wording of the questions. The student will realize that the self-completing questionnaire best suits the research on adolescent dating behavior because it is the most efficient and convenient way to gather the necessary data, and it best suits the private and personal nature of the subject.

Types of Questions

- *Open questions* require the respondent to answer the question in his or her own words, allowing an opinion or intensity of feeling to be given. For example:

"The relationship ended because:

_______________________________________."

These questions allow freedom of expression and have their place in more qualitative surveys, but they are difficult and time-consuming to code, and there is the danger that the researcher may misinterpret or misunderstand a response.

- *Closed questions* are more suited to a quantitative questionnaire. Discuss the main types of closed questions with the student.

- *Background questions* are used to gather demographic information, such as age and gender.

- *Dichotomous questions* offer only two choices. For example: "Did dating give you more confidence when meeting people?" (YES/NO), or "I feel that I have to act a certain way in a relationship because of my gender." (TRUE/FALSE).

- *Multiple choice questions* offer three or more choices. For example: "Where would you prefer to go on a first date?" (movie/party/walk in the park)

- With *ranking questions* the respondent is asked to rank each option that applies. This allows the researcher to obtain information such as relative preferences or importance. For example: "Please indicate, in rank order, the qualities that first attracted you to your date. Put 1 next to the most attractive through to 5 next to the least attractive."

  new car/popularity with others/fashion sense/self-confident manner/physique

- *Intensity, or Likert scale, statements* allow the respondent to express degrees of agreement / disagreement. For example: "It is important that my friends like my boyfriend/girlfriend."

  strongly agree/agree/neither agree nor disagree/disagree/strongly disagree

Point out to the student that it is possible to use more than one type of closed question in the questionnaire and discuss how and why; for instance, a group of dichotomous questions could be used at the start to obtain straightforward information, followed by a group of intensity statements to measure attitudes.

Types of questions to avoid include:

- Leading questions, or questions which presume the respondent holds a certain opinion or viewpoint, such as, "Wouldn't you agree that most teenagers are in a relationship by the time they are 15?"

- Questions which rely on memory. For example, "How long did you spend with your friends each day last week?"

- Long questions

- Vague, non-specific questions. Avoid words such as "regularly", "often", "rarely." One person's understanding of what is "regular" or "often" may not be another's. It is better to use specific breakdowns such as "more than once a week," "every week," or "more than once a month."

- Questions that use jargon or slang

The checklist for the questionnaire includes:

- Check that the questionnaire is clearly titled, with a sentence or two of explanation.

- Check that the questionnaire is clearly printed.

- Check that the questions are clear and unambiguous.

- If more than one type of closed question is used, make sure students understand the differences. Group different question types together if possible.

- Check that you have coded each question correctly. Coding is the assignment of a numerical value to each response in your questionnaire, enabling information collected to be turned into numerical data that can be quantified and manipulated statistically.

- Check the *reliability* of the questionnaire. This means that all questions are understood to mean the same thing by all respondents.

- Check that questions are in a logical order that makes sense to the respondent.

To minimize conditioning, general questions should precede specific ones. Group similar questions together. Place demographic questions (age, gender, etc.) at the end of the questionnaire. If you must use personal or emotional questions, place them at the end of the questionnaire.

Pre-Test and Pilot Survey

Tell students that before they deliver the questionnaire, they should carry out a pilot survey. There are a number of reasons why it is important to pre-test a questionnaire:

- To test how long it takes to complete
- To check that the instructions are clear
- To check that the questions are unambiguous
- To check the validity of the questions—are they asking for the correct or relevant information?
- To allow students to eliminate questions that do not yield usable or relevant data
- To allow students to test the coding of the questions

Tell students to pre-test the questionnaire on five or six people from the same population as the final respondents. After the pilot, students should ask their testers:

- How long did it take to complete?
- Were the instructions clear?
- Were any questions unclear or ambiguous?
- Did you object to answering any questions?
- Was the layout clear?
- Any other comments?

In light of any problems or comments from the pilot, adjust the questionnaire accordingly.

Gathering Samples

Ask students what some of the challenges might be in selecting the people to survey. Point out that unless a population is very small, it is impractical to have everyone in the population respond to a survey. Psychologists generally survey a sample of a population, which is a small number of people drawn from a larger population. Explain that for a sample to be useful, it must be representative of the population from which it was drawn. To help ensure representatives, psychologists generally rely on random samples, which are chosen in such a way

that every member of the population has an equal chance of being included in the sample.

For this topic, ensure that students understand the following:

- The survey population is adolescents.
- The questionnaire on dating behavior is to be filled in by 30–35 respondents who are a representative sample of that population. For convenience, all respondents will be students attending the high school.
- If the student were to obtain a list of all the students attending school and pick every tenth name or allow a computer to randomly select names from a database, this would be *random sampling.*
- However, gender is a variable, so the student must ensure a balance of male and female respondents. The list of names must be separated into male and female lists, and then an equal number of names picked randomly from each list. When a target population is divided into groups or strata, and individuals selected at random from each stratum, this is *stratified random sampling.*
- The student might decide that "adolescence" covered too wide an age range, and could be broken down into "early adolescence 13–15 years old," and "late adolescence 16–19 years old." This means the respondents are to be selected on the basis of predetermined instructions—in this case age and gender. This is quota sampling.

Ensure that the students understand the limitations and difficulties of random sampling. For instance, using schoolmates as the sampling population means defining adolescents as "teenagers who attend my school and live in my town." Point out that the views on dating behavior of suburban high-school adolescents might not be representative of the views of an inner-city adolescent or an adolescent working on a farm in rural America.

Once students understand the issues involved in administering the questions, they are ready to begin preparing for the questionnaire. Have students execute the following steps:

Prepare for the Questionnaire

- **Identify and research the topic.** Students should determine what information is needed and from whom the information may be obtained. Next, students need to gather available information on the topic from which to base the questions.

- **Prepare questions and structure.** To ensure the appropriateness of the questions, students should conduct a pilot survey. The nature of the questions will depend on the type of questionnaire being used.

- **Identify the population to be surveyed.** Students need to draw up the sampling frame and decide which type of sampling should be used: random, stratified, cluster, or quota.

Collect the Data

Discuss with students the importance of following the research design in collecting the data. Point out that different research designs require taking different factors into consideration. Tell students that, regardless of the method being used, they must carefully record the information because careless data collection can affect the accuracy of research findings. Note that students should follow these guidelines to collect the data using the questionnaire.

Conduct the Questionnaire

- Tell students that to ensure maximum response, they should notify all the respondents of the time and place they will distribute the questionnaire. For instance, students could make it known that the questionnaires can be collected in the cafeteria at the beginning of the lunch break on Friday. Ask for their return at the end of the lunch break.

- Respondents should be left alone to fill in the questionnaire. Not only would any contact with the researcher introduce bias, it would also compromise promises of anonymity and confidentiality.

- If not as many questionnaires are returned as were given out, tell students to resist the urge to go chasing after the non-responders—accept it as a limitation of the method.

STEP 4
ANALYZING THE RESULTS

Once students have finished conducting the questionnaire, they are ready to begin analyzing their data. This stage involves two steps:

- **Decoding questionnaire information and data input.**

This step involves using the coding scheme by which the students ascribed a numerical value to each response on the questionnaire in the preparatory design phase of the assignment. The students should have already tested the coding in the pilot study, so now they are ready to decode the finished survey. Ensure that the students know how to enter the coding values into the matrix of their statistical software or spreadsheet. Remind them it is essential they input the values accurately and that one entry error will invalidate all subsequent analysis. At the end of the data input, students should understand how the information from their questionnaire has been turned into raw numerical data and be ready to progress to the next step.

- **Statistical analysis of data.**

Discuss with the students how descriptive statistics can organize information and summarize patterns of responses; for example, the average age of respondents or the number of respondents who believe "companionship" is the most important element of dating. Show how frequency and contingency tables will allow them to make statements such as "43 percent of respondents strongly agree that friends' approval of their date is important" and "38 percent of girls and 21 percent of boys had casual dating relationships before they were 15."

Ensure that students understand the measures of central tendency—the mode, the mean, and the median—and appreciate the usefulness of being able to describe the data as a single value. It is essential that students understand that identifying and understanding the causal connections between events is a central theme of their research. Psychologists study cause and effect by examining the relationships among variables. A causal relation exists when a change in one variable—the independent variable— produces a change in another variable—the dependent variable. Ensure that the students are able to identify the variables involved in their own research.

STEP 5
PRESENT CONCLUSIONS

Once students have finished analyzing the data, they are ready for the last step in the research process—drawing conclusions from the data, testing the hypothesis, and representing the research findings to others. For instance, the students might conclude from their survey on adolescents' attitudes to dating that "teenagers feel that gender roles strongly affect their behavior in a dating relationship," or, "83 percent of boys claimed that dating increased their confidence in dealing with other people." Discuss with the students why they must show how they arrive at their conclusions and the importance of supplying supporting evidence from their research.

Assignment: Have students present the findings in a written report that includes the background and purpose of research, a literature review, a hypothesis, a research design (how the survey and questions were constructed), what the questions measured, how they were coded, problems encountered in the design stage, variables and measurement, data analysis, tables, graphical representation of data (bar charts or pie charts, for example), a conclusion, and sources and references.

Research Activity

Experiment

Before starting the activity, tell students that there are three parts to effective experiments: preparation and planning, carrying out the experiment, and experiment analysis and report. To organize, implement, and conclude their project, students should follow the five steps laid out below. While going through the steps, students should

- try to prevent their own theories, values, and biases from interfering in the research process,

- use careful and correct reasoning in drawing conclusions from their data, and

- carry out their research in an organized and methodical manner.

STEP 1
FORMING A RESEARCH QUESTION

Tell students that the first step in the research process involves selecting a topic for study. The focus of this activity is conformity, compliance, and obedience. For example, students might research the behavior of individuals in groups, peer pressure to obey or break social rules, or crowd behavior.

Once students have selected their topic, they will need to develop operational definitions of key concepts. Remind students that an operational definition is a definition that is stated in terms of measurable characteristics.

Review the Literature

Once students have defined their topic, they must research what other people have written on the subject. To determine how others have approached conformity, compliance, and obedience and what conclusions they have reached, students must review the published reports of studies that have a bearing on the topic. Discuss with students why good research is conducted within the context of an existing body of knowledge. Note that research will not only provide students with insights but also will help avoid duplication of research efforts.

Suggested readings for this topic include:

Asch, S. (1958). "Effects of group pressure on the modification and distortion." In E. E. Maccoby,

T. M. Newcomb, and E. L. Hartley, (eds.). *Readings in Social Psychology*

Zimbardo, P. (1971). "The pathology of imprisonment" *(Society)*

Aronson, Elliot (ed.) (1995). *Readings About the Social Animal.*

Sherif, Muzafer (1964). *Reference Groups; Exploration into Conformity and Deviation of Adolescents*

Milgram, Stanley (1974). *Obedience to Authority: An Experimental View*

Miller, Arthur G. (1986). *The Obedience Experiments: A Case Study of Controversy in Social Science*

Moscovici, S. (1985b). "Social influence and conformity. In Lindzy, G. and Aronson, E. (eds.) *Handbook of Social Psychology, vol. 2*

Blass, Thomas (ed.) (2000), *Obedience to Authority: Current Perspectives on the Milgram Paradigm.*

Moscovici, S. and Lage, E. (1976). *Studies in social influence. Majority versus minority influence in a group (European Journal of Social Psychology, 6)*

STEP 2
FORMING A HYPOTHESIS

After students have reviewed the existing literature, they need to develop a testable hypothesis. The hypothesis should be a statement that predicts the relationship between two or more variables. For example.

- Individuals will adapt their behavior to conform with that of others.

- People change the way they behave when they know they are being observed.

STEP 3
TESTING THE HYPOTHESIS

Tell students that the next step in the research process involves selecting their research design, or a plan for collecting, analyzing, and evaluating data. Point out that not all research problems lend themselves to every data collection technique, so selecting the correct research design is extremely important. Most of the data-collection methods used by psychologists fall into four categories: surveys, experiments, observation studies, and the analysis of existing sources. For this project, students will use the experimental method. Discuss with students the rationale of experimentation, the hypothetico-deductive method, and the key concepts of the classical experiment:

- **Experimental control.** This is the ability of the researcher to control the environment in which the experiment takes place and to control various factors—variables—relating to what is being studied.

- **Dependent and independent variables.** The dependent variable is the factor that the researcher seeks to explain, and the independent variable is the known factor that the researcher can manipulate or change to test the effect it has on the dependent variable. For example, in an experiment to test the effect of light on plant growth, the independent variable is light. By manipulating it (decreasing, increasing, removing) and observing the effect these changes have on plant growth (the dependent variable) conclusions can be drawn about the relationship between the two variables.

- **Causality and correlation.** Causality means that two or more variables are so closely related that when one changes, the other also changes, or one *causes* the other to change. In the plant/light example, the conclusion based on observing the relationship between light and plant growth might be "light causes growth," a conclusion that would allow predictions to be made—"plants would not grow in an absence of light." A correlation, on the other hand, is an observation that two or more things occur at the same time, that is, the variables change, but a change in one does *not necessarily cause* a change in the other: it may be accidental or coincidence.

Compare the use of the classical experiment in the natural sciences and the social sciences. Ensure that students understand the difficulties faced by those who seek to apply classical experimental rules to the social sciences. For instance:

- Natural science deals with easily manipulated objects, but people have consciousness—they are aware of the world around them and can act purposely towards that world.

- There are ethical, practical, and methodological problems that make classical experiments less common in the social sciences.

- All experiments involve the manipulation of independent variables in order to measure the effect upon a dependent variable, but the large number of possible variables involved in social action makes it is difficult to establish causal relationships and to accurately repeat an experiment for the purpose of verifying data.

- Standardizing the conditions or environment under which an experiment takes place is problematic when investigating social phenomena.

- Experimentation in social research is more likely to be contaminated by unforeseen factors. Illustrate this point by discussing the Hawthorne effect.

Discuss the instances where laboratory experiments have been used in the social sciences. Ensure that students are familiar with the social psychology experiments of Asch, Milgram and Haney, Banks and Zimbardo. These should be discussed critically and if students choose to develop similar experiments, advise students of the limitations of such a line of research.

Tell students that some researchers have overcome the difficulties presented by classical laboratory experiments by conducting field experiments, which take place in the real world and those involved do not realize an experiment to being conducted. For example, if students wish to test the hypothesis that "people behave differently when they know they are being observed," they might observe and perhaps record people in a social setting covertly one day, then overtly the next, noting changes in behavior. Point out that field experiments may have problems of their own, such as the inability of the researcher to be aware of, let alone be in control of, all possible independent variables without setting up a wholly artificial environment.

Why Use an Experiment?

- It allows researchers to test a hypothesis under controlled conditions.

- It may provide insight into aspects of behavior.

- It allows students to explore the differences between natural and social sciences

Operationalizing Variables

Discuss with the students the importance of precisely defining the variables. Operationalizing variables means defining variables in terms of how they will be measured. For example, if an experiment is designed to measure changes in conformity by a subject's choice of line length, then the operationalized definition of "conformity" as a variable should include the concept of line length. Impress upon students that operationalization is central to the experimental method.

Prepare for the Experiment

- **Identify the topic.** Students should determine what information is needed and from whom the information may be obtained.

- **Research the topic.** Students must gather information on the topic on which to base the experiment. Students should be familiar with the work of Asch, Milgram, and others.

- **Design the experiment.** Students should detail the set-up of the experiment and the context within which the independent and dependent variables operate. Students should address a number of issues:

  - the independent and dependent variables—why they were chosen, their operationalizations, and how the problems of subjectivity and bias will be minimized;

  - experimental control—how procedures will minimize threats to the internal validity of the experiment by bringing the behavior studied under control and holding it constant;

  - sampling—who will take part in the experiment (individual or group) and why and how they were chosen;

- pre-test—students should run a small scale pre-test of their ideas to see if they are practical.

Collect the Data

Discuss with students the importance of following the research design in collecting the data. Point out that different research designs require taking different factors into consideration. Tell students that, regardless of the method being used, they must carefully record the information because careless data collection can affect the accuracy of research findings. Note that to collect the data in the experiment method, students will conduct the experiment following these guidelines.

Conduct the Experiment

Have students follow the bulleted points:

- To obtain meaningful results, the student should not vary the set-up or administration of the experiment between cases.

- A minimum of 10 cases of the experiment should be carried out.

- Results should be recorded accurately and consistently. Where possible, recording devices such as a video camera ahould be used. For instance, where the student is examining the changes of behavior under observation, video filming will not only supply recorded information on behavior. but it will aslo serve as an obvious indicator of observation to the subjects.

STEP 4
ANALYZING THE RESULTS

Once students have finished conducting the experiment, they are ready to begin analyzing their data. As a class, discuss why the analysis of the data collected is an important step. Point out that even if students used the proper research design and carefully collected data, the accuracy of their findings can be affected by how they analyze the data. Tell students that as researchers, they must be careful to maintain their objectivity and not read more into the data than is there because research findings are only as good as the methods used to collect and analyze the data. Remind students that the purpose of their data analysis is to determine whether the data support their research hypothesis. Psychologists use a wide range of statistical methods, many of them very complicated. Students of psychology, however, can interpret a great deal of psychological information if they have basic understanding of a few statistical concepts.

To analyze the results of the experiment, students should understand how descriptive statistics helps to organize and summarize data, and should understand the concepts of frequency distribution, contingency table and, most importantly, the measure of central tendency—the mean, the mode and the median.

For example, if the student finds that in 10 instances of an experiment, the number of subjects who responded by changing an element of their behavior is 5, 6, 8, 3, 4, 9, 2, 3, 7, 3, the mean—the mathematical average—is produced by adding all the values and dividing by the number of instances—50/10 = the mean is 5.

The mode is the value around which the greatest number of observations are concentrated, or, more simply, the most frequent observation. In the case of the figures above, 3 occurs 3 times, so the mode is 3.

The median is the middle observation in a data set, with 50 percent of observations occurring above and 50 percent occurring below. In the case of the data set above, the median is 5.

Ensure that students know the value of being able to compare statistical results and make generalizations about the data. Once students have analyzed the information gathered in the interview, they should prepare a summary of the information.

STEP 5
PRESENT CONCLUSIONS

Once students have finished analyzing the data, they are ready for the last step in the research process—drawing conclusions from the data and presenting the research findings to others. Students need to examine the wider issues and implications their experiment has revealed. Investigation of the shortcomings and drawbacks of experiments is as valuable a line of inquiry as examining the successes. As a class, discuss why psychologists generally report their findings in professional journals, in scholarly books, and at professional meetings. Point out that by reporting their research findings, psychologists add to the body of psychological knowledge and make it possible for other psychologists to evaluate the data and the research process. Note that when psychologists do not supply enough information to allow their research to be repeated by other psychologists, the findings are often viewed as spurious.

Assignment: Have the students present the results of their experiments as an oral report.

Before starting the activity, tell students that there are three parts to an effective case study: choosing a suitable subject to study; carrying out the study and carefully collecting data; and analyzing the data and preparing a report. To organize, implement, and conclude their project, students should follow the five steps laid out below. While going through the steps, students should:

- try to prevent their own theories, values, and biases from interfering in the research process,

- use careful and correct reasoning in drawing conclusions from their data, and

- carry out their research in an organized and methodical manner.

STEP 1
FORMING A RESEARCH QUESTION

Tell students that the first step in the research process involves selecting a topic for study. The focus of this activity is the family. Specifically, students might want to investigate parenting styles or the effects of daycare on children.

Once students have selected their topic, they will need to develop operational definitions of key concepts. You may need to remind students that an operational definition is a definition that is stated in terms of measurable characteristics.

Review the Literature

Once students have defined their topic, they need to research what other people have written on the subject. To determine how others have approached the study of the family and what conclusions they have reached, students will need to review the published reports of studies that have a bearing on the research topic they select.

Discuss with students why good research is conducted within the context of an existing body of knowledge. Note that research will not only provide students with insights but also will help avoid unnecessary duplication of research efforts. Reviewing the literature may also help students redefine their topic or limit the scope of their research. Encourage students to make

appropriate adjustments as they work through the seven steps.

Suggested readings for this topic include:

MacDonald, Judith B. (1994). *Teaching and parenting: effects of the dual role.*

Bornstein, Marc M. (ed.) (1991). *Cultural approaches to parenting.*

Amundson, Kristen J. (1989). *Parenting skills: bringing out the best in your child.*

Clarke-Stewart, Alison (1982). *Daycare.*

National Council of Welfare (1988). *Child care: a better alternative.*

Schiller, Judith D. (1980). *Child-care alternatives and emotional well-being.*

Wright, Caroline, and Jagger, Gill (eds.) (1999). *Changing Family Values*

Coontz, Stephanie (1997). *The Way We Really Are: Coming to Terms with America's Changing Families*

Leira, Arnlaug (ed.) (1999). "Family Change: Practices, Policies, and Values" (*Comparative Social Research*, Vol. 18)

STEP 2
FORMING A HYPOTHESIS

After students have reviewed the existing literature, they need to develop a testable hypothesis. The hypothesis should be a statement that predicts the relationship between two or more variables. Case studies are qualitative research. Typically, the case study researcher does not look for generalized cause-and-effect relationships, but places emphasis on exploration and description. However, in this case, a hypothesis provides a convenient starting point, although the student may want to modify it as the case study progresses.

Share the following examples of hypotheses with students:

- Daycare tends to inhibit children's emotional and intellectual development.

- Daycare generally improves children's emotional and intellectual development.

- A strict parenting style helps children feel emotionally secure.

- A permissive parenting style is useful for helping children to feel emotionally secure.

STEP 3
TESTING THE HYPOTHESIS

Tell students that the next step in the research process involves selecting their research design, or a plan for collecting, analyzing, and evaluating data. Point out that not all research problems lend themselves to every data collection technique, so selecting the correct research design is extremely important. Most of the data-collection methods used by psychologists fall into four categories: surveys, experiments, observation studies, and the analysis of existing sources.

Case Study Method

The case study can be said to fall within the same category as observation; it often takes place in a natural setting, such as a private home or classroom, and seeks to interpret the meanings of the behavior under study as it occurs in the real world. A case study attempts to provide as comprehensive an understanding of situations as possible through *thick description*, a process which involves an in-depth study of the subject, the nature of the community, the characteristics of the surrounding people and places, and the meaning of the social context, including cultural attitudes, norms, values, and attitudes. Unlike the quantitative research methods, the goal of the case study is not to amass numerical data, but to understand situations, and the complexity of social processes that influence them, in a real-life setting.

The researcher must decide on the type of case study to carry out. There are four subdivisions:

- **Illustrative.** These are primarily descriptive studies, using only one or two instances of an event to give a general impression what a situation is like.

- **Exploratory.** These are short pilot studies, conducted before commencing a larger scale study. Their main purpose is to test out types of measurement and identify questions prior to the main investigation.

- **Cumulative.** These accumulate information from multiple sources collected in the past in an effort to understand more without the expense of a new study.

- **Critical Instance.** These studies examine information from one or more sources for the purpose of studying a unique situation. They have no interest in making universal generalizations about it.

To obtain as complete a picture of the subject as possible, case study researchers often use more than one research method, usually chosen to correspond to the six types of data collected in case studies:

- **Documents.** These could be letters, records, reports, memos, and so forth.

- **Archive Records.** These include such items as diaries, maps, and charts.

- **Interviews.** One of the most important methods of data collection, interviews can be open ended, allowing the subject to give opinions; they can be focused and limited to a particular topic, or structured, if a formal, quantifiable survey is required.

- **Direct Observation.** This may occur casually during a site visit.

- **Participant Observation.** The researcher actually participates in the situation being studied, despite the danger of bias.

- **Artifacts.** These are physical evidence gathered as data. Examples are notebooks, pictures, and computer output.

This *multi-modal* approach also serves to increase the reliability and validity of the data. Case studies are likely to be more convincing if they are based on several information sources.

Why Use the Case Study Method?

- It provides an in-depth examination of an individual or small group.

- Behavior is seen in its natural setting and can be directly observed.

- It is a flexible method of research with an emphasis on exploration rather than prediction, allowing the researcher freedom to address unforeseen situations and to reshape the original guiding questions.

- By specializing in thick description and using more than one data-collection method, the researcher can compare the interpreted data to information collected by other methods.

Advise students that the information-rich interpretive nature of case study research that makes it so flexible does have a downside, however. Case studies are sometimes dismissed by researchers for being too subjective and unscientific, too reliant on the researcher's interpretations, too difficult to test for validity, and too rarely offering any problem-solving solution. Add to this the fact that it is the most expensive research method—and in the end, all for the study of just one or two subjects—and it is not surprising that psychologists tend to treat it with suspicion.

Tell the students that the case study activity for this method is to choose a friend, classmate or relative and carry out a case study over a period of time. This will involve regular contact to collect the data, an examination of the subject in the context of home and community, and interpretative analyses of data. The guiding question will be the hypothesis on the family.

Researchers try to make sense of the data holistically or through coding. Holistic analysis tries to make some sense of the data as a whole, but researchers, using coding, sift through the data to categorize specific characteristics or actions which then become key variables. The researchers use a number of analytical frameworks to organize data:

- the role of participants
- the analysis of formal and informal exchanges
- thematical
- historical
- resources
- ritual and symbolism
- crucial incidents that challenge fundamental values

By coding characteristics into the seven frameworks, the researcher can look for patterns among the data and the patterns that give meaning to the case study.

Once students understand the issues involved in the observation method, they are ready to begin their observation. Have students execute the following steps:

Prepare for the Case Study

- **Identify the topic.** Students should determine what information is needed and from whom the information may be obtained.

- **Research the topic.** Next, students need to gather available information on the topic from existing sources.

- **Identify the subject to be studied.** In this case, a subject chosen by the student suitable for extensive case study.

- **Determine the type of case study to be undertaken.**

Collect the Data

Discuss with students the importance of following the research design in collecting the data. Point out that different research designs require taking different factors into consideration. Tell students that, regardless of the method being used, they must carefully record the information because careless data collection can affect the accuracy of research findings. Note that students should follow these guidelines to collect the data for the case study method.

Conduct the Case Study

- In the case study method, the student will be compiling "deep data," which typically include documents, letters, print-outs, notebooks, pictures, tape recordings, case study protocols (conversation recordings), and so on. Despite the disparate nature of the records, they must all be filed and coded carefully.

- Instruct students to keep a detailed field diary to regularly record observations and to keep a schedule for meeting the subject.

STEP 4
ANALYZING THE RESULTS

Toward the end of the case study period, the student should begin coding the data. Using the seven frameworks and a measure of judgment, the student should begin categorizing the information, and, at the end, interpreting the result, giving reasons for the decisions at each step of the research process. To draw all the data together, the student should compile a case study report. Boerher (1990) says of the report "a case study report is generically a story; it presents the concrete narrative detail of actual, or at least realistic events, it has a plot, exposition, characters, and sometimes even dialogue." Some reports include the reactions of the participants to the study.

STEP 5
PRESENT CONCLUSIONS

Once students have finished analyzing the data, they are ready for the last step in the research process—drawing conclusions from the data and presenting the research findings to others. Bearing in mind the initial guidance hypothesis of the relationship of the subject to the family, the student should address that relationship in the report. Case studies are often exploratory and most conclude with implications or recommendations for further study.

Assignment: Have students prepare and deliver an oral presentation to the class. Ask the students to explain how the advantages and disadvantages of the case study method affected their research.

ACTIVITY 9

Statistical Analysis

Before starting the activity, tell students that there are three parts to statistical analysis: identify the topic to be examined, collect the data, and analyze the data. To organize, implement, and conclude their project, students should follow the five steps laid out below. While going through the steps, students should

- try to prevent their own theories, values, and biases from interfering in the research process,

- use careful and correct reasoning in drawing conclusions from their data, and

- carry out their research in an organized and methodical manner.

STEP 1
FORMING A RESEARCH QUESTION

Tell students that the first step in the research process involves selecting a topic for study. The focus of this activity is the prevalence of psychological disorders in modern American society. Students might research how many people in the United States suffer from schizophrenia, depression, or an anxiety disorder and whether these persons are under the care of a mental health professional.

Once students have selected their topic, they will need to develop operational definitions of key concepts. You may need to remind students that an operational definition is a definition that is stated in terms of measurable characteristics.

Review the Literature

Once students have defined their topic, they need to research what other people have written on the subject. To determine how others have approached the study of poverty and what conclusions they have reached, students will need to review the published reports of studies that have a bearing on the research topic they select.

Discuss with students why good research is conducted within the context of an existing body of knowledge. Note that research will not only provide students with insights but also help avoid unnecessary duplication of research efforts.

Reviewing the literature may also help students redefine their topic or limit the scope of their research. Encourage students to make appropriate adjustments as they work through the steps.

Suggested readings for this topic include:

Mathew, R. (ed.) (1982), *The Biology of Anxiety*

Hollandsworth, J. (1990), *The Physiology of Psychological Disorders: Schizophrenia, Depression, Anxiety, and Substance Abuse.*

Kleinman, A. and B. Good (eds.) (1985), *Culture and Depression: Studies in the Anthropology and Cross-Cultural Psychiatry of Affect and Disorder*

U.S. Department of Health and Human Services (1999), *Schizophrenia*

Warner, R. (1995), *Schizophrenia*

STEP 2
FORMINNG A HYPOTHESIS

After students have reviewed the existing literature, they need to develop a testable hypothesis. The hypothesis should be a statement that predicts the relationship between two or more variables.

Share the following examples of hypotheses with students:

- Most Americans who suffer from schizophrenia do not receive professional treatment.

- Depression and anxiety are much more common in American society than schizophrenia.

STEP 3
TESTING THE HYPOTHESIS

Tell students that the next step in the research process involves selecting their research design, or a plan for collecting, analyzing, and evaluating data. Point out that not all research problems lend themselves to every data collection technique, so selecting the correct research design is extremely important. Most of the data-collection methods used by psychologists fall into four categories: surveys, experiments, observation studies, and the analysis of existing sources. For this project students will use the analysis of data from existing sources.

Existing sources (or, as they are more often called, secondary sources) of data range from highly quantified sources such as statistics to more qualitative sources such as personal diaries, business and academic reports, historical documents, newspaper articles, or television programs. For this activity, the student will be using existing statistical data.

There are many potential sources of statistics: businesses, the media, universities, and interest groups all produce information that can be used as sources of statistical data, but the source of data that is generally considered to be the most important to the psychological researcher is the government, which produces what are known as "official" statistics.

All modern societies need information about their populations in order to formulate social policy and its levels of expenditure. Government departments and agencies regularly collect large amounts of data about state and national trends in areas such as employment, public health, education, and so on.

Psychologists use official statistics for a variety of reasons. Firstly, on a purely practical level, the cost in money and time to conduct large-scale surveys may be unfeasible when such data already exists. Secondly, the use of official statistics may be a necessity if comparative or historical research is being carried out. Thirdly, some forms of official statistics, such as the census, are produced by surveying every household in the country—as representative a sample of the population as possible. Discuss with students the reasons they should use official statistics for their research on psychological disorders.

Why Use Official Statistics?

- They are produced regularly and are freely available to researchers in an easily accessible form.

- They are produced from large-scale comprehensive and representative surveys that would be too expensive and time consuming for psychologists to carry out.

- They may be the only available source in a particular area of psychological interest.

- Using official statistics drawn from a number of different years, it is possible to examine changing trends and conduct "before and after" studies.

- Official statistics can be used for comparative studies—for example, to examine differences in types of treatments for psychological disorders in different countries.

Problems Using Official Statistics in Research

Tell students that although there are good reasons to use official statistics in research, there are also a number of problems.

- **Problems of control.** Psychologists are not involved in producing official statistics and so have no control over the design of the survey or the process by which the data has been collected. For example, government surveys are structured to meet official, specific objectives, not to meet psychological criteria.

- **Problems of definition.** The definitions used by collectors of official statistics may not be the same as those used by the psychologist. For example, official definitions of effective treatment for a psychological disorder may differ from what many mental health professionals believe.

- **Problems of bias.** Although official statistics are presented as objective, unbiased facts, some psychologists point out that these statistics can be biased. For example, a government's definition of a particular disorder might be written in a way to justify a level of funding for research of the disorder.

Once students understand the issues involved in using official statistics, they are ready to collect the data.

Collect the Data

Discuss with students the importance of following the research design in collecting the data. Point out that different research designs require taking different factors into consideration. Tell students that, regardless of the method being used, they must carefully record the information because careless data collection can affect the accuracy of research findings. Note that to collect official statistical data, students should follow these guidelines.

- **Collect the data.** This may consist only of accessing the relevant statistics
- **Interpret and evaluate the data.**
- **Report the findings.** Include a statement of the problem, review of source material, assumptions, research questions and methods used to obtain findings, the interpretations and conclusions, and a thorough bibliographic referencing system.

STEP 4
ANALYZING THE RESULTS

Once students have finished collecting data, they are ready to begin analyzing the data. As a class, discuss why the analysis of the data collected is a very important step. Point out that even if students used the proper research design and carefully collected data, the accuracy of their findings can be affected by how they analyze the data. Tell students that as researchers, they must be careful to maintain their objectivity and not read more into the data than is there because research findings are only as good as the methods used to collect and analyze the data. Remind students that the purpose of their data analysis is to determine whether the data support their research hypothesis.

Remind students of the problems inherent in official statistics: problems of lack of psycho-

logical design, problems of definition, problems of bias. Point out the problems associated with surveys that may affect the analysis. For example, the wording of the questions might be ambiguous or unclear, especially to ethnic groups whose first language is not English. Discuss the possibility that questions might not always be answered truthfully and the difficulty some surveys have in gaining the cooperation of certain groups. Point out that statistics are a tool for organizing and comparing large amounts of data and that all information should be interpreted with care. Once students have analyzed the information gathered using official statistics, they should prepare a summary of the information.

STEP 5
PRESENT CONCLUSIONS

Once students have finished analyzing the data, they are ready for the last step in the research process—drawing conclusions from the data and presenting the research findings to others. Point out to students that the use of official statistics has many advantages as a research tool, but drawing conclusions from an uncritical use of such a tool may involve many practical and methodological problems.

Assignment: Have students present the findings of their research on psychological disorders in a written report.

Presentation

Now that the students have completed their research activity, collected the data, made an analysis, tested the hypothesis, and drawn conclusions, tell them the final step is to prepare their findings for presentation and assessment. Tell them that no matter how rigorous and thorough their research, its presentation is critical; even the best research will be wasted if it is poorly presented and inaccessible or difficult to follow and incomplete. Remind students that the purpose of research is to add to the body of psychological knowledge and to allow other researchers to evaluate the data and the research process. To facilitate critique and research reliability, the student must present all the information necessary and follow the conventions of how the work is presented.

STEP 1
FORMING A RESEARCH QUESTION

Tell students that the first step in the research process involves selecting a topic for study. Have students pick a new topic to research, or ask them to expand on the research they have done for an earlier research activity.

STEP 2
FORMING A HYPOTHESIS

After students have formed a research question, they need to develop a testable hypothesis. The hypothesis should be a statement that predicts the relationship between two or more variables.

STEP 3
TESTING THE HYPOTHESIS

Tell students that the next step in the research process involves selecting their research design, or a plan for collecting, analyzing, and evaluating data. Point out that not all research problems lend themselves to every data collection technique, so selecting the correct research design is extremely important. Most of the data-collection methods used by psychologists fall into four categories: surveys, experiments, observation studies, and the analysis of existing sources.

STEP 4
ANALYZING THE RESULTS

Once students have finished collecting data, they are ready to begin analyzing the data. As a class, discuss why the analysis of the data collected is a very important step. Point out that even if students used the proper research design and carefully collected data, the accuracy of their findings can be affected by how they analyze the data.

STEP 5
PRESENT CONCLUSIONS

Once students have finished analyzing the data, they are ready for the last step in the research process—drawing conclusions from the data and representing the research findings to others. Have students follow the guidelines below while preparing their presentations.

Written Presentations

Written reports should:

- have a clear layout
- have headings and subheadings
- be organized around key points
- have concise, clear sentences
- be free of jargon
- be spell-checked
- be proofread by a third party
- have all math double-checked
- be double-spaced
- have an extra line space between paragraphs
- follow the layout present below:

- **Title Page**

Tell students that this should include the title of their research project, their name, their teacher's name, and the date. If their project has a course title (Research Project, Community Assignment, Module 8, and so on) this should also be clearly stated.

• Contents Page

This clearly lists each section of the research, giving the number of the first page of each section.

• Abstract

An abstract is a brief summary of the research. It states the aims, the research method used, and the conclusions drawn. This gives an at-a-glance summary of the research.

• Background and Purpose

To introduce the report, this deals with the general area of interest and the specific topic chosen to research. Why was this particular problem chosen?

• Operational Definition

Remind students that an operational definition is an expression of a variable with measurable characteristics. For example, an operational definition of a double-blind study would be "an experiment in which neither the participant nor the researcher knows whether the participant has received the treatment or the placebo."

When the term in question is conceptual, such as giftedness, it must be operationalized and made measurable by the addition of indicators. So, the operational definition of gifted might become "children with IQ scores above 130 or children with outstanding talent for performing at much higher levels than others of the same age and background."

• Literature Review

This should be a substantial section, demonstrating familiarity with a range of books, articles, and papers in the chosen field of research.

Tell students that they should be able to identify:

- the main stages and developments of the field
- the main issues, controversies, and problems
- the main texts and personalities
- the main methodologies and approaches
- the context into which the student's work will fit

This section should contain a critical evaluation of the literature. The student should not limit the reading to the suggested book list, but should also search relevant journals.

• Hypothesis

Following logically from the literature review comes the hypothesis. Students' hypotheses should suggest a relationship between variables and be expressed simply in one sentence.

• Research Design and Methodology

In this section the student will describe and justify the choice of research methods.

- What method of primary research was used?
- Was the study quantitative or qualitative, or a combination of the two?
- Were any secondary data used?
- Why use interviews rather than questionnaires? What was the benefit of one method over the other?
- How was the sample chosen?
- Were there any problems? If so, how were they overcome?
- Were there any ethical considerations? How were they dealt with?
- How is the work valid?
- How is the data reliable?

• Data Collection

An account of the data collection goes here.

• Data Analysis

A brief description of the statistics involved is given here.

• Presentation of Data

Where appropriate, students should present numerical data in the form of graphs, charts, tables, or diagrams, and

- include a descriptive title
- label all variables and measurement units
- show the independent variable on the horizontal axis
- show the dependent variable on the vertical axis
- indicate the source(s) of data
- show statistical tests under tables
- show the number of observations (N)
- indicate if using percentages

• Conclusion and Recommendations

Tell students that no new information should be added in this section. The conclusions should be drawn from what has already been presented and discussed. If the students are making recommendations for future research, this is where they should appear. They should make specific references to their hypothesis, issue or research questions, and their aims, noting whether their aims have been met.

• Evaluation

At this point students will evaluate both the outcomes of their research and how successfully it has been carried out. Students should take an honest look at the research process and ask themselves: How well did the planning and time management go? What could be changed for future projects? Was this a positive or a negative consequence? In what way?

Explain that evaluation is an important skill, and encourage students to consider how well they have developed their evaluation.

• Bibliography

The bibliography will list all the books, journals and other sources that have been used for reference. A list of other sources used purely for background reading can also be added.

Students should format academic papers and journal references this way:

Thomas Sweeney, "Operant Conditioning: New Findings," *Journal of Behavior* 34 (2002): 6–18.

• Appendices

Appendices should be used sparingly. A good use of an appendix is to include a copy of a blank questionnaire or set of interview questions. Anything presented as an appendix should be referred to within the study, usually in either the presentation of data section or in the main text.

Oral Presentation

Tell students that presenting the outcomes of research orally needs to be given careful planning time. The student needs to think not only of the clarity of delivery through voice levels and diction, but also of the visual impact made on the audience. Students will need to consider how best to present work and allow time to prepare for it fully.

Students will normally be told in advance to how many people they will be presenting their work, and how long their presentation is expected to last. A slightly short, but clear, interesting presentation which demonstrates preparation, and knowledge and understanding of the subject, together with enthusiasm, will be assessed more highly than a long-winded presentation demonstrating little preparation or forethought.

Students need to know where their presentation will be held. This will help them decide how loudly they need to speak, where they will position themselves, and how far away visual resources will be from their audience.

Advantages of an Oral Presentation

Assure students that an oral presentation should not be seen as extra work. It is an integral part of the research process and an important skill. Oral presentations promote personal development in many different ways. Giving a presentation helps to build self-confidence. It allows researchers to demonstrate their skills to their peers. This can have the effect of bringing individuals closer together through a mutual understanding of the need for support and the sharing of new ideas. Oral presentations may seem daunting, but people often surprise themselves by how well they perform.

Visual Resources

An oral presentation needs a focus. This is usually of a visual nature. There are many different resources that students can use. Students should almost certainly include some of the following:

- overhead projector transparencies
- presentation software, such as PowerPoint®
- audio-visual resources (tape recorders, videos, slides)
- tables, charts, and graphs
- handouts

Overhead Projector Transparencies

These useful transparencies offer the opportunity to exhibit information to the whole group at the same time. They also avoid the need for anyone to be looking down at a handout or sheet of statistics while the presenter is talking. Tell students that this encourages the audience to listen more carefully and to think about the subject area.

Transparencies need to be written clearly or typed in a large font size (16 point size is a useful size for small group presentations; a larger size should be used for larger groups). The following is a useful checklist for successful transparencies.

- Clarity of typing or writing is vital.

- The size of type or writing needs to be suitable for the size of your group. Use different colors to break up the text.

- Restrict the amount of information on any one sheet.

- Include only the main points of what you are saying, or use the transparency to present supporting material.

Presentation Software

Microsoft's PowerPoint® is a software presentation tool, akin to a "slide show." It enables students to present their visual material directly from a computer, replacing overhead projector transparencies or photographic slides. With PowerPoint they can move text and merge images during the oral presentation, eliminating the need to change transparencies, refer to diagrams on posters, and so on. It can be set up to run automatically, or under user control (for example, the user clicks on a mouse button to activate the next presentation slide). For this to be a successful means of presentation, a good understanding of how to use PowerPoint® is important, and reliable equipment is crucial, as a technological problem at the last moment could mean an end to their presentation.

Audio-Visual Resources

Students may feel it is appropriate to use a short piece of video footage within their presentation. The relevance of anything shown needs to be very clear to the audience. It needs to add something to their talk to be of value, and should not be used if the topic could be explained just as effectively without it. It is important that video equipment is set up in advance and is ready for use. This includes finding the right place in the footage so that the presenters do not keep the audience waiting while they search for it.

The same guidelines apply to slides and to audio tapes. Audio tapes will need to be clear for them to be of any use within a presentation.

Before student presenters use any audio-visual material in a presentation they need to be sure that they are not breaching any ethical agreements of confidentiality or anonymity. Always be certain that permission has been obtained to use the material.

The following is a useful checklist for successful audio-visual resources.

- Audio-visual resources need to be directly relevant.

- They should add something specific to the presentation.

- They should be set up, ready for use.

- They should be of good quality. This is particularly important with audio tapes.

- Be sure permission to use them has been given. Never breach ethical agreements.

Tables, Charts & Graphs

If the students need to include tables, charts or graphs within their presentation, they are best set out on an overhead transparency. They might like to back this up further with the use of a handout, to be distributed at the end of the presentation. This will enable the audience to continue to consider the content of their presentation at a later time.

Handouts

Tell students that a handout is a sheet of information relevant to the presentation material. Handouts can be a useful way of consolidating the understanding of the audience by giving them material to read again at a later time. Handouts need to be clear and inviting to read, not too crowded with information, and directly relevant. It is important that handouts are given out after the oral presentation is over. Giving them out beforehand could distract their audience, who might be tempted to read them through rather than listen to the presentation. A handout should back up the information they present orally, and offer opportunity to extend it further. Always ensure that there are enough for all those present.

Assignment: Have students present their findings in a written report. They may want to include visuals such as charts or graphs in their report. Then have students give oral presentations of their reports.